The Hermit
IX

Venus Grimm

ISBN:

DEDICATION

me

CONTENTS

...

Hi-Bye Conversations

Death Child

Short Stories

Solitude

Miscarriage Awareness

~ for those who are lost, this will find you~

And that's what it feels like. Magic almost.
To find something written for you in a time you most relate. Almost as if you wrote it yourself, the words flow from another as if they picked your brain miles away

HI- BYE
CONVERSATIONS
{when it's in the way you talk}

Push
I fell in love with the push

It doesn't always take a gut feeling or my intuition to just know you're no good. I got standards on top of expectations on top of highs of emotions that can be less clouded than the smoke you blow out. A smoke that you tilt your head back to blow up to the moon while the rain hits the window. A smoke that covers the tears filling your eyes but still causes you to try to pass it to me. I'm currently setting emotional boundaries. My body is tired of the pain and stress of simply talking to people that are just hi and bye company.

I am without a Coven.

However, I wonder if I ever had one. I've spent my whole life, every move, every new school, every lost friend, as just a "I'm here for education" and "finding myself" without ever craving to find a place to belong. A woman can dream though. Having hopes of coming across fellow spiritually guided people where we can come together and share knowledge/ practice like witches. Male or Female don't make no difference I just want someone who is like me to find me and we can run away and live life together. A body of peace that will push me as much as I push myself and pull to be around me spiritually, emotionally… physically.

Yet as I know where to look it's a commute to get there and until then I'm stuck in the "hi" and "bye" company under the world's cloud of smoke.

Do Not Disturb

IX

She'd never complain
Never cry
Never crave that you could see how every time you claim to love her, her heart would die
She knows you'll never read the rant or hear to conversation she has with her girlfriends
Even if there was an instance that she'd show it, you'd be too slow to notice- but listen to me she's at peace with not talking to you
Not worrying about what makes you move the way you do
And someday I hope that you know how much she did love you
But in that messed up head of yours she hopes you can see how much you didn't love her
You lied and begged for her to see that you did because perhaps you might have been able to convince the little roaches you traded her with that this treatment is "love"
But you never backed up your words
Always pushed her away to handle everything herself and never once cared for her to stay
You didn't give effort so she will find better
You will find another and perhaps you will learn and change
But take accountability of the faults you made

Space

It's the space
Space is a place in which people meet and think they are trying to get to know my soul
Soul like mine but without actually talking about real shit
Shit you say that turns into a "good morning, how'd you sleep" and "wyd."
"Wyd" can't even spell out truly "what are you doing" you just leave it as the acronym
Acronym you hide behind to show you can't even give me the time of day
Day you spend to say to me something less than a phrase in hopes for me to stay
Stay when I'm not given space just meaningless words through a person who won't change
Change without me having to say every time that's not how to speak
Speak right to a woman like me who walks in her soul
Soul that she hopes someone could in line with her naturally out of control

Autumn Talks

You ever just sit up at night and listen to the rain. Thinking of a masculine energy to hold you through the pain. All I ever had was my own to treat my femininity like a queen. When I said I didn't love myself it was myself who said I was being too mean. Said here's what we gotta do so that I can not get stuck like people do. In the beginning I could barely trust the healing I threw myself into. And now I'm constantly falling into love with the only person who hated me enough to help me up.

IX

If you have control, then command the sky to rain and roses to bloom.
When then, and only then, as the command works can you call it yours.
Soon you might understand that they belong to the earth because you
cannot command the movement of something that doesn't belong to you.
Something that you are a part of is earth. People are to coexist not take over
the other things living in this world. They are to coexist- we're not over.

IX

Did they leave you staring out a window wondering if your dad would ever show up? Or did they leave you with a mom who could never say she loved you?
both, perhaps.
I wish you grew up thinking that you were enough

IX

Forgiveness is a battle

The only way to get over them, is to forgive what made you get under them in the first place

Forgiveness is a medicine
The only way to stop hurting is to forgive those for poisoning you with things you trust were safe to receive

Forgiveness is a release
Not a quick one- but necessary to pull you out of the dark trenches or trauma that's trapped you in your mind. Pain holding down your body like chains to a wall because you won't realize that you have had the key to unlock them this whole time
You'll learn to grow patience and will to leave your situation. So, you won't go down without a fight but wait- it's not just them, you easily could have been a problem too or not that's justifiable to you

Forgive yourself for being the problem
Forgive yourself for being the one that went through forced upon pain
Hurting you won't get them anything but empty chairs around their grave
But hurting them because you were hurt won't get you anything but the same.
Let them go
They already took too much power- all you have to do is want it back

IX

I do live outside the drowning thoughts.

You're my words

Ideas flowing through my right brain through the fingers that hold the power to recite what's in the mystical world in my mind. Left on paper either as a draft or final copy.

Always from the heart.

The mind to express what's dying or living in the world is planted in all but activated in few. To express different ideas or invent a narrative out of blood. Red pouring out the mouth from poison in another's heart.

Or red- pumping chemicals of serotonin to bring out a smile that will become something someone can read about later. Either way, it's a way of expression. What I do that is. A way to feel less arcane perhaps… that's what being a writer means to me

IX

You make him nervous
If he looked in your eyes long enough he'd flutter like the butterflies
So, he glances away
If you watched him dance, he'd have two left feet
Trip and fall when you ask him to be-

Relaxed is how he feels too when y'all decide to talk
His mind takes breaks but just can't stop
Thinking maybe you could be why- maybe not
Tells himself to stop for his heart can be quiet dark
In the end he's not trying to say anything out of the ordinary

Perhaps he can just cherish the time y'all have
Perhaps he can love the delusion he created wanting you more than a friend
Knowing you feel nothing yet-
Knowing you feel nothing at all

IX

Let me be
When you love a flower you don't pick it because it will die
So let me be as I am to the earth
I know who I am- what I need
I got soft because the universe told me with it I'd find my peace
Not because of those who tried to pick me
Don't let my peace make you think the grass I grew in was green
Let me be

IX

She's worth the dimes spent
The time dropped to stay and see her-
Body she communicates like the air
Smooth but in terms of the earths' rasp

Reads energies like seasons
Switches power like air pressure
She moves with the hurricane rain
Loves with a disguised autumn soul

Unique in the power she holds

IX

{Death Child}

IX

The music playing seems to be quieter than the thoughts that race. For once it may feel like you're out of place wondering if you ever mean anything to the world. Believe me- the world has conditioned people to find a purpose. To marry. To have sex… but darling I know you just want to be loved without the chains.
You might want to find a group that you can be comfortable with. Or even just one person you can actually call a friend.
But you can't find that… so instead you find ways of taking yourself out of this world because you don't feel worthy to continue living.
I'm not going to sit here and tell you to stay. You don't need to find a way to relate.
But if you care to continue to read then might I ask you something…

Are you really ready to go?

IX

Burden

Blood drips down my wrists with curiosity
Stains from the cuts to my thighs like pure beauty
It never rushed down like the tears from my painful nights but it was running down. No two people can live the exact same days but many feel too much of the same pain. A knife I used after using the average cardboard in my five prior years to inflict pain. Wondered what could do the trick but didn't want the scars to make my future self-sadder than I already knew they'd be.

After all, if I wanted to give the scars, I needed to be ready to show them off. Didn't want to have to hide the bruises as much as I already did my suicidal thoughts. So, I just tested shit and played until I realized I couldn't not leave a mark. The anxiety that once held me back felt no longer held by the "what ifs."

Then I sat in the bathtub one night. Water slowly climbing up my neck as my body slid in more to my control. Thought to myself…

"Do you really want to die in this place?"

Location

She came to school the next day in bandages. Quiet like her tongue was taken yet her eyes showed she was too stunned to speak. Memories of red dripping over her tub traced her brain.
We planted our seeds but only my tree survived.

She came to school but didn't make it home. Caution tape lined the bathroom that was closed the next day. Rope had reached from the ceiling and grabbed her by the neck, but nothing was there to assist her in catching a breath.
We too planted our seeds but only my tree survived.

He went to sleep one night and never woke up. Blood didn't stain the pillow, instead the sink but there was an empty bottle on the nightstand. Now he's just a figment to the broken minds.
But the seeds he thought didn't survive now sway with him again.

The Souls

Those who chose to free themselves from the pain return to the world in peace. Now spirits, angels or omens planting the long-awaited seeds to feed their own souls and live without the chains that tied them down. It hurts to watch the one you love go away. Hurts to know that they couldn't bare to stay so you start to inflict blame on them or yourself.

Before thinking their "weak" or crying because "why would they leave me?" consider their side of why it was simply not worth it to stay. Not everyone can learn on earth how to tend the garden of their soul. Not everyone's blade that cuts them is dull.

IX

Flash

Life is full of choices. Some people drown themselves in the bottle. Others pop candy pills to not stay awake. More rely on the clouds that they blow from their mouths to share the secrets of their lives fate. Yet many just hold onto the hope that one day they will be saved- healed. However, as we are all our own beautiful souls, not everyone was given the gift to heal themselves. It surely takes strength to decide whether to leave or stay. It is a choice that will hurt either way.

Last time

The stars in her eyes hold more secrets and love than she would ever tell. Though the sweet smile that promised forever was taken along with her.

Why didn't you finish your explanation?- you never answered

We lived in fear but we had each other. I guess you just gave up on us. They said you would be fine but your body had already soaked everything in. Our fingers intertwined while tears poured down my face. I watched as the line went flat. Now the only thing I can hold is the last words you had said:

Forever was us
"I love you"

Time

An estimated assumption of how long something may last. Not promised. Just an hour or day you can look forward to in the future. Or a point you can mark from the past. Yet invented with importance from sailors and businessmen… most just cared about the general as a sense of telling the day and seasons to get by.

So- why does my time matter if not taken in my own hands?

Technically no matter how much time someone tells us we have it will never be enough, now will it?

Even people in their older age get scared to die because it isn't until you realize your biology clock is slowing down that the inevitability of death becomes real. And the living people in your life will soon wake up to spend the rest of their days without you. Living days you never got to share and going places you'll never get to see.

I guess my question is… how do you want to tell time before you reach deaths inevitability?

IX

You look tired

Pain in my eyes
Grey or invisible bags lie
Voices in my head hide
Try to tell my secrets in unescapable cries

Grow with no regret
My heart tries not to fret
When this soul was never full
Broken cracks are red for the bull

IX

Rain continued…

Moons out thunder shouts for places he finds comfort
Walk through a dark house for spots you wait you dastard
If he might fright, blood goes high, his eyes could lay upon you
Where y'all could stare out the window while rain hits so gentle
Until he comes to miss you

The difference was he didn't see blue
Life was only red for you
So, music became your separating game
100 loud in your ears it plays

His cry wakes your blue inside
Perhaps his patience can help your red color change
To something that might allow you to let him stay

IX

Drugs

It was almost instant
The relief
For once I felt my thoughts and pain leaving the internal box
Poof- magic for my brain
Now it crosses my mind these days
Maybe I should do drugs?
Drink a little, eh?
I mean how could it be
Just for a short while anyway
Not enough to get addicted

IX

She knows-
It was bound to happen. Felt like she wasn't fully in control. Drew blood but that doesn't make her a monster for being curious. Her brain runs for miles since she was clean for years. Mental health feels like it's worsening sometimes then flips to being better. She's in a creative high- doesn't feel the need to sleep or eat. Just yearns to learn new things and colors.

She's trying because she still loves herself with every vibration in her body- every beat of her heart. But it's not about love… it's about care and not judging herself for what she had cut or may cut again.

Curiosity killed the cat
(but isn't there more to that phrase?)

IX

Challenge

Feet slide gently in the clear blue water. The glow of orange in their petaled feet shine under the moons lights while crickets and owls begin their nightly music.

Taking deep breaths as their soul moves the matter around them in seconds before they release their vines. Impatiently sliding down her shoulders from her head to take a dip.

They giggle softly standing up. Walking into the water with their head held high. Rocks press into the drift below their feet just before they dive in. A glowing object lights the bottom attracting them to sink towards it.

Controlled, they head into the deep. They didn't come to resurface.

"13 ways to what is good"

Bend to their will
Let them hold the key

A single smile will set me free

Don't talk back to the one who's house you live inside
They speak and you obey
Listen clearly
Even in spewing hate

My soul is pure to help
Those in need will be good

Qualities that please me

Honest like the rain
Open like the wind

Well balanced but to who?
Your eyes look at me -blue-
You cry so I comfort your side
Nice equals good in their eyes

Smile, laugh. Don't let them beat your ass
Stand up tall. Don't let them fear you at all
Cry but try. Help

Treats me nice, and asks 21 questions
Looks around for me when near their presence
But laughs and smiles, doesn't push my boundaries
Thinks about decisions

Never crossed my mind
Her loving me in a days' eyes

IX

Bloom a new soul
A new trial to behold
One with no secrets & holes
One with no fear or goals

A cape over shoulders will define you
Save a girl and the world is yours
A crown on dark mind will scare you
Burn the world for a girl & it's hers
Now to be either one has its faults
To be anything other than true you too
But for the girl's best interest, what do you choose?
Catch her in a fall… or burn the world?

Who told you that you had to?
Sometimes you convinced yourself "I should"
When you wanted to be everyone's "good"

IX

"Sometimes you have to be someone else to hear
the voice of reason"

Period

I was told once that I was mysterious and worth getting to know
But at what point is too much
At what point will you look at me like: "I'm finished" because I opened up about all identities and the things I love are now in your brain
At what point do you think it's rather annoying to see me in this way?
Holding you like you're the only one I ever want because you truly are…
We talk about our hopes and dreams, a bathroom door dividing us because my cycle started and you're too scared to buy products from the store
When is too much knowledge, too much?

Do you want to get to know what keeps me up at night as we share the same bed, a ring on my left hand, and no regrets in my heart but what about in yours?
Would you sit here and watch my heart break as you leave the place we call home all because you didn't define to yourself what you actually wanted to know about me?
Here… let me make it easy for you to understand… is it my mind or my body you want to know more?
Do you ever sit down and think about knowing the real me?

IX

Bite Me

Broken dreams through broken eyes
I told myself that one time

Yet as I lay awake, in pain hoping to not see a new
fate, tears fall down my face with the power of an
earthquake

I-I see you there
Your eyes all glared

So, the covers quickly flow over my hair, head in
the pillow, as I tell myself "relax" on repeat
Music playing loud in the background

Something you learn is that the fall may be more
anti-climactic than the climb

IX

Talking to the voices in my head makes me think
twice. They won't take you seriously until you take
yourself serious- but some people will always find
a way to pull you down

Power to control

It's in power that someone can control you.
Manipulate you
Bend you at their will to do what only they may
desire.
Don't let someone have control over you
Easier said than done yes but the thing is you
decide how much that person can control you
Who can and if they can put you in your place

Perhaps

Sometimes I feel as if life is a pit of nothingness. A sense of senses put in your head and pulling at your heart. Sometimes I live the days out to the fullest and others I pull on strings trying to control myself before fully collapsing. Left out and forgotten or never given air to breathe.

I don't completely hate life. I just hate the days where life isn't yours anymore or that grasp is ever so slipping away.

IX

Darling it's okay to be upset

It's okay to let your emotions show

"just don't act out"- says everyone you know

But fuck what they know

It's okay to want what the world hasn't given you yet

IX

… I feel your nails in my back. If you're gonna hurt me hurt me…

IX

Perspective of a survivor

You touched me…

First my shoulders then my legs in areas that once belonged to me.

You touched me…

Now shaken in my bed, my eyes opened all red, but you didn't care what I said…you felt me…

Before any lover could

Before a child understood the painful impact of a- "No" you miss understood for a "yes."

Silenced.

Covered my mouth so crying didn't slip out. Wrists held to the ground. Why did you touch me? You vaguely explained before putting me in pain. 7,9,10,11, and 12 in my age. Now you sit here and pretend you didn't want me in the end, I was lost, hurt, and bent in ways you pointed out. Let's pretend you didn't hurt me so now we're friends, but I can never forget. I'm older, lying in my bed, visions, and thoughts still in my head.

Don't even cry as I feel the breath against my skin, my stomach turning, it's just a memory of losing myself once again. I didn't give my body it was stolen at a young age. Over and over told what happens in the house stays in the house and sadly… you're not the only person who wanted to taste.

{part two...}

Your hands cold against my thighs, my heart beating faster trying not to lock eyes. My mouth covered by your hands, I was told to stay silent and did.

That's probably why you liked me though?

- Innocent
- Naïve
- Always did what I was told

Though it's the aftermath no one talks about. The tears I cried, the times I lied, the amount of days spent throwing up the morning after worried I was pregnant too many times… until I stopped fighting. Just took it keeping my thoughts busy over the years.

Soon you got bored. Didn't try anymore for I had gotten stronger. But those nights I couldn't sleep. Constant running that made my legs weak… you would hover behind me. I'd shake as you touched my shoulders, whispering in my ear while your hand found its way around my back.

You'd say: "meet me in the room" because there are too many people around anyway, but they could never hear or see my cries for help. I soon learned to never ask. Having to brace it on my own. It's almost as if they were blind but blame, I will never put on them, for it was more than my heart that felt pain.

So, when you ask why I choose not to trust, I trained myself to believe that if a guy wants it, he will take it, can't get it he will break it and if he likes you he will say it. I don't have to do anything to get a guy's heart, to corrupt his thoughts, to make him do secret things in the dark.

Because as a child I didn't have to do anything for multiple guys to touch my body parts.

IX

…E Adesso?

Stunted my growth

IX

Feels like a never ending ride

Blamed. Abused. Tortured for every mistake that she made. Constantly she wished for me to have not been born let alone as a daughter. Neglected and lied to in the name of "that's what mothers do."
When I think of her, I think of pain. Being blocked out of my life only a button away. Using everything against me and taking me for granted because she married the wrong man. So big on communication but can't talk to her kids.
A financial struggle was never what it was, but the money was held over my head like I ever asked for dollars. All I wanted was to be loved and to feel safe, but she threatened my life, cornered and pushed me into walls to sit in "a child's place."
"I love you"- she never said
"I'm proud"- never was in her head
"I'm here" was never in action
"bitch"- rolled off her tough like a first language

I hope she learns to grow up and take accountability.
In the end it never mattered the words I'd say. The conversations I'd hold with her and the emotions I expressed as she voiced how much she simply could only give me hate.
In the end I've accepted and forgiven the blood that makes her my mom.
And in the end…
Blocked out my life is only a button away.

I'm done talking to the woman who can't help but call me a bitch
Guess she got the doctorate but human decency couldn't be teached

IX

Just stop…
I can't keep swallowing the pain that you won't take accountability for

SHORT STORIES
OF THE WORLD

Closure: A social justice memoir

[... Somebody give me a sign, I'm starting to lose faith ...]

The world moves slowly around them, the streets lighting up from the sun's glare, not letting the bright fire hydrant that the kids play around barefoot take away from its own shine.
Left glancing around at the different shades of brown held on the skin of those in this world who have been shunned to staying away from those who don't possess high amounts of melanin.
No people that's skin is a light winter mood insight, reminds those that segregation in housing isn't ending
For their only hope is in the book of a god they call their father.

Housing segregation lasted from 1880 to 1940. Another problem on our list is that we can't hide in the afro spotted a distance away on our heads. I gaze upon red and brown as I wince into the mirror, breaking yet another comb in order to try and prepare to house hunt with my mother. Taught not to come off as "too black" for the two-story home and fenced yard for a dog that's not a pit bull.

We drive past the once graffiti-filled streets and sounds of gunshots I once called home, in a neighborhood that the government left to rot but was saved by the Aunties in recent years. Reminisces of my vague childhood merge with the new profound understanding that struggle will all be over once I reach my judgment at the end of the road. Carefree. Hair fluttering in the wind, braids bouncing softly, as a child runs along the streets in the road trying to beat the street lights from coming on so their grandmother will allow them to play outside again tomorrow like I once did many years before.

[Look, I been through so much pain and it's hard to maintain any smile on my face...]

A white room, inside nothing but the body of a toddler me, stands sitting in space. Wondering who they are or what even they are.

Feet touch the gravel hard as the street light comes on. Not enough air filling my lungs while my own braids plan the betrayal of how to distract my eyesight. My home in view. Slowly fading pavement into a new rough texture. Still don't know my name. The days and seconds don't pass as normal but with the ever so soft ticking sounds, I feel my brain become anew. Back inside the room, pitch black until I was given the freedom to see the world in a consecutive time frame. To have room to call my own and a place to return home too… Home.

--- *all my dreams turned into nightmares* ---

Madlock plays on the old box tv screen my grandma possesses (as do many other shows on distant channels). The white picket-fenced houses and pale skin are noticeable under the pearls that lie on their wealthy necks as they solve yet another mystery. Graffiti and gunshots being the only thing that brings light to my people in the rural cities that once were full of job opportunities but now gang violence that everyone seems to fall into. Although the world is ugly, we can be more and do more than being defined by the color of our skin. Yet the white picket fences only are in pale homes and green neighborhoods, not the ones around the children watching lack of representation on VHS tapes while only looking at the possibility of a location in the clouds that can give one eternal life.
Or at least happiness off of Earth.

I see the actors on the tv in front of me praising their god for the creation of everything they now know. Wondering why they find it so hard to believe that other people don't have the same end goal as they do, looking up at the clouds…

[…Cause there's madness on my brain. So I gotta make it back, but my home ain't on the map…]

It is a long drive through the crippling memories of what was once told to me: "What are you really going to do with your life, that's just a hobby that won't pay the bills" which later turns into "never give up but never try either" in the eyes of those who take care of me. Hands press gently against the soft back of the bible. "Amen!" my mother says once again, as my feet guide me up the stairs quietly. Trying not to make a sound.
She yells my name ready to start another long conversation that will provide little to no insight on anything relevant. That's not my name but rather a name you gave to me at birth.

"Yes," I whisper back, preparing for my doom.

Mom and I only had one good religious talk about a song: Montero (call me by your name) by Lil Nas X, and during that, I had been able to define my own sense of belief. After all… the only reason many of us are stuck in our heads as children is that our parents told us right from wrong. But when the glass heart shatters and you're left crying, alone to pick up the pieces over the years, I straightened my back one day, put pencil to paper, and decided to fight my battle.
Starting off with rewiring the cords and rusted drive that was burning in my parent's control.

IX

"Where do you see yourself?"
"I want to live in an apartment."
"That's a waste of money. Not a nice place to raise a family."
-silence-
"You can't make living with an apartment as your goal. You need a house plan," she says to my brother again as he sits at the dining room table.

The smell of cooked chicken and broccoli filling my nose as the sensation of multicultural music pumping through my ears drowns out the sounds around me. We now have a new house but have not been accepted yet. "It's a process," the people say.

My brother doesn't respond to my mother's previous statement.
She continues explaining the "American dream" forgetting that the American dream is rather nitpicky and distant in what is defined as American. It's not personal but rather a program put in the heads of all of those who can't get it. At least that's how I see it, see… refrigerators had been invented in 1913. The public was now wanting that convenience but most had been denied that luxury solely because of income and backhand skin. Then the "grass yard" dream was evolutionary to the American dream. So now that peer pressure to prove that you have wealth over self-worth corrupts you just enough so that the other soccer moms and football dads can get jealous of your "new life."

While parents smile, kids cry in the corner from childhood neglect. Chained to the door with tape over their mouths, as your pearls shine brighter than their rags against their skin. People think they are gods because they have tons of money. Power over the hearts and minds of others who have a buck less in their hands.

[I need the (memory). In case this fate is forever. Just to be sure these last days are better]

The hair that once fluttered in the wind, curls now fluff of the eyes, as a noceur child walks along the walls of her house. Ducking and tip-toeing in broad daylight listening to music to ease her aching heart.
Avoiding outward communication.
Finding themselves prone to Oneirataxia more often than not.
They want to live in the clouds. To control the weather and be closer to the soft kisses of the rain.

--- *I go to sleep. Trying not to be scared at the thought that I won't wake up tomorrow* ---

Tacenda

IX

***Bebe Rexha, Machine Gun Kelly, and X Ambassadors. "Home" ***

Dedication

IX

Her name, which is quite unknown, will make anyone feel arcane. She stayed at the bar every Thursday. Sat across my counter. I'd clean glasses and poor other people's drinks. A few people judged her but she never cared what others had to think for her eyes would flood like not cutting off the kitchen sink. She just wrote in her little book as if she was waiting on someone. Glancing left to right, looking at the clock then the door. She had let out a deep sigh before she smiled one day. Tipped me for nothing as the wind carried her away. Even though we only ever talked about what was going on in the world. All through this "keeping her updated" I had found her to be my everything.

Do you wonder why I wrote this in the past tense?

Probably not, no one ever cares… but her. She had no friends, lost them all and was now lonely. Scared now to not know or do things that everyone else did so she was always writing, always looking around, and always on her phone. But I used the past tense because it was the past. What we were that is. However, the blood that runs from my words still runs under the rope around my neck. The tears from her face are equally stained like the carpet she sits on under me.

IX

Social Media selection

A ghost lurking under those messages, able to go unnoticed behind the mask, can almost switch through it naturally
Waking up and going to bed everyday just going through the motions trying not to… *click*… looks back into the mirror… *click*… looks still in every picture but lively in videos. Those videos that once were lively but won't be around within a day. No matter how hard you try we will always find you. How come I can see what you do?
But unlike others I can see the smile fade once the camera doesn't- *click*… They're pretty aren't they? The girl who owns the account you stalk every day. Aesthetically a good color composition and internally the same. You are perfect to you when a filter crosses your face because you are told beauty is symmetrical and your face is not symmetrical. But as long as that fire and those hearts continue to be poured next to your pictures, you're told you will feel whole. But do you?... 24 hours… the buzz is gone… a ghost lurks under the messages.
A different face to be seen.

IX

GRIMM

Roll green dice, lands on a three, you look into my eyes. Are you watching me?

We know now is your time, eyes all puffy and wide
I'll let you go, slide, this one little time
So, you can get your things, before your last goodbye-
"One more chance, let me deal you your soul. I feel a little generous if it's the truth you hold."

My feet stop at the door, hope in your eyes as I hold the dice… six being prize.

"Is your goal to trick me? If it's not today" and you stare at me in an awful way.

"My heart is pure," you say, I reply:
"Like the souls trapped in my eyes?"

You now swallow your pride. I kind of like it this way. I smile faintly before saying: "you have one day."

"Grimm oh Grimm, might I fight for my life?"
"It's not mine to give."
"But it's yours to take."

You should have watched your words; this is a promise you can't break. With the pain in your eyes, I sign then shake the dice.

"We can play until the last star leaves the sky."

Grimm Part two:

"Hey, you said I had one more day?"

"You're not my only patient, might I say. I like you but I got to run. The sun's pointing light to a new whose soul I must greet."

"Do you expect me to just wait? In a dark room, I hadn't eaten in this heat."

A smile of yours triggers mine: "Care to join me while the last star sits in the sky?"

With subtle emotion you stand up. Gentle to the touch as you stare at me with a straight interest.

"Now my acquaintance don't get addicted, I am quick to lose interest-" but I smile and decide: "I haven't done this in a while."

"Have a partner in crime."

"Yes, one with no souls in their eyes."

"Getting souls is your life prize?"

"It is now since I died… but I preferred the simple things when alive."

"Like staying up late at night to clean bruise and scars you thought wouldn't heal?"

You grab my hand. I look upon it before meeting you still grey eyes. Your sky is paling, haven't you noticed, it's out of my control that you will die.

"I have my own. Myself and I."

"But you don't have to."

"You have one day."

"Aww don't treat me this way."

I know you can see me, no one can these days, and I am not soft to humans but you are quite arcane.

"It's not like that brought you here, you know?"

"Yes, but it's death that gets to keep my soul."

"And when you leave, where do you want to go?"

"To wherever **you** find home."

IX

Red shoes

Alone in the dark. Gray to white spectrum without your touch to bring me color.
I cry.
Maybe it's the look that you once held in your eyes after all I said was goodbye, but it angers me. Almost as much as the swaying leaves next to me on this street that we walked, back when you had a heart beat that healed my inner thoughts. I miss you…

'Breathe me'

Zoning out to music, a playlist we created, our heads would bob in sync. I miss you…

'Breathe me'

The version of you I can never get back. All you saw was red. A knife under the pillow on our bed, the very last song that played in your head… caused my white shoes to turn red.
It was me or you and…

'Breathe me'

Deep down we both knew… falling in love will cause us to fall hard in the dark, I should have killed you from the start of the spark. When your smile took my broken heart, when you lied to my face and didn't change your ways. I am angered from a bitch and controlled it because I know how to stitch. Now I still wear these red shoes that were once only white to you.

Marigold

I don't desire it, no, lately, but my brain does think of it. So, surprise me, maybe, but ask first of course. Your arm around my tors-o can't stay still for my giggling keeps filling the room. Laying on my back, your stomach unlike mine can handle the placement. Wrapped my legs around you in the basement.

It's a hug, you pushed me down, apologized so I wouldn't frown but I pushed you back because I do attack and we can fight with no long distance making it easy to come back. So, you fell on your back, and on your legs, you slowly pulled me down by my chin, so that you could whisper softly "I want to take care of you."

It's not like I'm surprised but to let you in like that, I could possibly be open, yes. My heart beats in my chest but I don't want to run before our night's rest.

"I don't know, I want it to happen naturally, I guess."

"You said you'd feel it, a feeling I know at best."

"We've never kissed." I sigh as I rest my head on your shoulder.

"And we've never had sex," your mumbled words hit my chest. You lift my chin up softly, my heart bangs my lungs as your smile lights up the room.

"Moon or sun, you're my best friend and I will always want you for you."

"What about-"

"No."

You interrupt the tears falling from my eyes. Yours water: "Flower just don't think about it. Is it so wrong for me to want to see you at your best? I understand what you are guarding-"

"It's not wrong" my words croaked and broke. "But just like you we both have a fight, and anger that if we take this route, death of the other will leave us broken."

My tears to be first are now stolen as one of yours runs down your cheek, hitting my hand it was destined to meet. I touch your face concerned "didn't mean to make you hurt. I just-"

You pull me closer with your eyes. Arms wrap around me as I climb onto your lap for a better position, our foreheads touching with forgiveness.

Hand now on the back of my neck our single tears come to a rest, "You're a lot Flower but I want you. By choice and energy I give you my protection. But will you give me your hand to hold when the darkness grows and we will share ideas until we grow old?"

"I know you know it but love is pain and this could be hard."

"Who said I didn't like these healing scars?"

I smile and nose laugh as we keep our eyes closed.

"Don't test my love."

"For love is the crazy kind right?" I reply.

Then you pull something out from behind you, a flower. A marigold...

Rings of Grey

Rain pours bringing Persei's long red-grey hair strands to a wavy melt, matching the rings of the aged tree trunk she sits on. She runs her finger along the circles like she did her wife's hair while drinking tea. Pondering life that just three weeks ago wasn't this lonely with her Normay who was lost in the silence. Laid there still and when that tree fell so did she. Persei wasn't home so she sips tea and thinks–if she fell due to sickness laying near the tree that's now a stump, did she make noise in the empty woods when no one could hear?

Either way Normay is at peace. Peace because of old age. The only thing needed to fear was losing Persei and she never got to live a day without her in the end. Persei looks up at the sky with her eyes closed thinking of Normay's hands wrapping around to hold her now breaking heart. She remembers her grey strands of stress that showed up because of Normay's years of work. The adventures of camping and building their new forever home as they traveled the world in a bus while young.

"Live long enough to have your stories be your foundation. Everyone gets grey hair but not for the same reason," Normay would say as her and Persei sat on the dock.

She'd brush her hair.
"I'm not insecure of my grey. Each strand tells a story."
"Of stress," Normay would laugh.

Persei kept her warm smile.
"Well that and because you have lived long."

She runs her fingers along the rings wincing in pain, grabbing her chest. Trees have seen so many seasons and created so many homes in all their years growing. But Persei's grey hair of old age and secret stories now are their own tree rings that are to be left behind.

Persei mouthed, "I'm coming to join you in the sky."

She felt an arm wrap around her, as a voice replied, "I'm sorry but I'm happy to see you died."

Apricity

Hands, soft, wrap around my back to hold me up. Dipping me but won't let me fall as we dance under the moonlight. Scents of roses and marigolds fill your eyes. You look at me like I am all you want. Those eyes I lock onto, hold me in close like the previous conversations of big cats we had while watching the Jungle book.

I love it like this.

My pencil drawing the flowers as yours the birds above. Ending our night with the soft grass in our backs, laughing at the amount of times we start back at one. Neither of us can keep track of the stars. Fingers of ours intertwine as you rest between my legs, head on my stomach rubbing my thigh as I do your hair. Careful not to mess up the curl pattern. Asleep, my eyes close with the last words you say: "We'll never be far apart." Our eyes may close but our hearts remain open. Ready for the new day.

This is the idea, yes. I wish that when my eyes creep open, I'd soon be able to feel you. See you in the apricity with blankets around our backs. Ready to embark on a journey.

A journey unique to us.

One to never be alone again.

IX

Sleeping Sci-FI

The stolen blankets sprawled on the floor are warm for once. A yawn now forced out of him; he sits down facing the rest of the room.

Never turn you back on it

His feet then legs find their way under the old grey blanket that is now stained with blood. Dried like the well near the outhouse he used in grade school after practice.

"Did you hear that?" he ask aimlessly, looking at his own hands. No one is near to respond. He forgets that he is now all there is left.

The sound of the rain hitting the metal roof rings in his ear. Helping him shift his emotions of tiredness to fear for the short moment of realizing that something sounds to be nearby. A crash outside like thunder roars but the landing is more comparable to a dog than a cat.

The sun's not down yet. He has some time. He flips the blanket back over his head, trying to control his breathing so he can head back to sleep.

A loud growl comes from in front of him. Creeping closer as the door begins to creak… "please fall asleep- please" he begs in his own inner monolog. Something then proceeds to lift up the sheets…

Never turn your back on it

Innocent Fear

Fear's mom used to call fear special because she was born afraid from day one. Her mother kept Fear's fright under control and gave her comfort from everyone's opinions. Until the day came and strangers went and took her mom away. Told fear that monsters lurked in the shadows and pain in the heart. She was afraid for many years that followed that day. An orphan lost and abandoned without her mother's comfort. Left to be paranoid out of control.

When I first encountered Fear she was sitting on the sidewalk with her knees to her chest. Rocking back and forth whispering what you'd perceive as ghostly chants. A whiteness spread over her face as the wind whistled.

"Don't be such a chicken. It's wind," her friend Bravery came running up exclaiming with two cups in his hand. Unlabeled as if illegal.

"Well let's hurry before the storm picks up," she rolled her eyes.

Heading back to her dark bear cave she calls home. I ducked behind a wall so she wouldn't see. Pondering the thought of why she slept in a home so dark. She fears everything like roaches and the storm's rain. But she fears what cuts deep like the pain of being alone since losing her mom left her with a grieving heart. Forever searching for someone who can understand her fears. Her mother used to say, "There's nothing to fear for there's a rainbow behind every storm" while rocking Fear to sleep.

Some people say Fear is cautious and delicate. Many say she is paranoid, and others say she's the reason they sleep with covers over their heads. Scared that if they look out their window at night, they will find her standing there.

Whispering in their ear- "Do you see a rainbow?"

SOLITUDE
{not lonely but alone to live how I please}

IX

Sometimes I daydream about laying on the roof of my own car
One that can hopefully take my weight as I feel the colors of my heart
Run around in circles looking for more space
Hoping that if I found a nice place I could learn to stay

Sometimes I have nightmares that I won't be able to sit
Have trouble wondering if I'd be able to sleep when my car is my only home
If I lived out a suitcase, I could find more peace
Driving around the world flying to my beat

Sometimes I see the orange of the tapestry on my walls
And I ask myself do I fear the climb more than the fall
It makes my dark room happy when I look up and see just one color
For sometimes I just can't help but wonder

Wonder if I'd make it to finally discover my favorite color… of me

IX

She's soft like a last name change left to create a new identity yet she's wild. Like a risky photoshoot or a path that lovers fall into when the leap of faith gets strong enough. It's forbidden arcane words you're trying to erase. But she's soft… so very soft, in the skin, leaving your brain to spin because you're not trying to fully dive in just invite her to hangout and hold your body. So don't blame her for lacking the "we'll last forever" innocence when you ask her to let you in.

She is constantly hurt by the world, trying not to give up because she just wanted to be a choice in love someone will continue to make. Now she fell hard into peace finding that someone to be herself.

IX

I rather just live in a car, prepare to go off grid, write my fingers weak and sell shit at flea or artisan markets than work like this to pay the bills of society

IX

A home is inside where you put up the lines
Telling the world you can't cross here since my soul is mine
My home is in the elements
In the universe
In my self-made walls
My home is not in a person because the foundation will fall

Talk to your house

Day: 6606

Trick of treat me with love me even in pain to show you that forgiveness will wash it away. I'd rather fall in myself than break the fall than break without the connection of my soul. I want you because you deserve more than temporary peace. More than a love that leaves you stranded in your sheets. I lay with you until the sunrise to set to rise and I want you to know I still got your back till you have officially closed eyes.

Expect rain around 4pm

I cried then a storm came

Rain dances against the gravel. My fingers lay in the stream going down the drain. Rain hits my back softly. My hood over my head so my bonnet won't get wet. My bare feet feel the temperature of the warm driveway.
I get up to dance under the sounds of thunder and lightning above in the sky. It pours hard to silence my cries and the thunder teaches me to breathe in with no fear.
Now as the rain gets lighter with my tears, I sit against the house. Clothes drenched and smiled slightly. Happy that it rained today.
My face to the sky as a few cars pass then two birds come back. Thank you, thank you once again- I'm happy the storm came.

Treasure

"What's my most treasured possession?" I was asked.
Where I answered, "My body and my soul."

The two things that are tight and I would never sell for gold. It's funny because sometimes I think that I will never have a first when you have to touch my body well to get to my soul- let's rehearse:

When two brains race a different mile on the same track it feels like power. Feels like lavender filling the room as you step out of the shower. Then it all feels like pain, in an overwhelming and wanting to face way. That type of pain that makes love turn the others way.

Even when two brains seem to connect for a moment on the same path, there will be a time where they go separate ways. Yet my soul is the balance and my mind and body sit on the scales.

It's not my soul that titter tots the balance in love. It's my attraction over mental interaction that will test if you pass or fail.

Day: 6343

The feeling I'm feeling is understandable. Like a shift in energy, I didn't want to go through. Maybe it's that I have a lost reaction to things that don't bring me vagary.

Try to push me farther than I am, and you won't be given any chance. Want to grow with me but I'm not letting you solve my mystery when you can't seem to understand that you need to match my wavelength of maturity before you can come with me to fly.

Empty

Alone and worried I can't focus on that now. Empty thoughts roll through my head, not surprised I can't move my pencil… how when the world crashes down and we are again far apart. Could you let me tell you my secrets in the dark. Under moon light, not pitch black we were crazy from the start. But you know that. You always did know how to get in my heart.

To show you my true feelings I must open up-
But what if that box isn't empty enough?

Numb

I don't feel too lonely
I like being alone
All of me is worried that I won't be able to create my home
So many things I love are falling out of place
Seems like nothing wants to fill the spots- taking stops
Tired of being around people
Tired of pretending like I'm not-
Crying myself to sleep seems as normal as my dark skeleton thoughts
Numb to the feeling and list of--} what makes you happy when not?
Left to saying "I don't know" because my brain is tired of explaining my thoughts

Running Water

Poofy earth grown hair pushed up under my blue hoodie
Warm water rushes over my barefeet
Running down the drain at the corner of this street
Sand and brown dirt underneath

The street is smooth
Water fills the visible cracks
Thunder rawrs, now there's no going back
I can feel my spirit getting it's sense of relief

My thoughts laying back to bite the peace

I notice the black tube sticking out the wooden wall
Water pouring down it like a water fall
I smile getting close to it
Proceeding to wash my hands and feet

I said aloud before touching the rushing water-
"I wish it would rain."
Now my hair is soft, slightly wet
To the press of a poured down hoodie on my head

The world it seems unnatural, yet the thunderstorm is home
Thank you, universe, for helping me feel I belong

Home

With that, I don't think my soul was born for this world.

Under the longing to travel and never feeling at home, my soul was born somewhere else, placed in this human body. Now subjected to following American rules.

Bills, Bills, and taxes.

I just want to exist, and this world is tough for that. Things are expensive and I can't travel without worry or fear of my life or overspending.

Health care is a big oof in my check along with the things I need like water, food and breathing- lil asthma check.

I just want to go off the grid and travel. My best morning person days were when thirteen-year-old me only had Pinterest. Spent most of her days getting s A's, writing songs, poetry and staring at the stars through the window. Finding home in the sky while leaning against her bed photographing the sunset.

Feet in the air.

Flower

A flower
Symbol of love
Symbol of romance
Along with death
Something can have so many different meanings,
impacts too, but look the same
Yet you still hurt yourself. Bully yourself looking
for one meaning when in reality, just like a flower,
you mean so much more

It doesn't always matter when
But as you grow into loving yourself try to think
of your thousands of different meanings. Only
you can decide how you are defined

See… one meaning will bring you joy
The other pain
Maybe fear and a high chance of truth

Don't be scared to listen
Don't be scared to dig into your youth

Define Feminine

Define feminine
A woman, alone, now ready to cut her hair

Lead to believe that her curls were to be tamed
But they are just as wild as the animals outside
Similar to her soul
Her curls have their own control
And eventually the shadows will just cross over
But she can only be insecure if she doesn't secure herself

For that the road is getting easier to see
To let what defined her whole life just not
To break free from what hid the insecurities
Reach the final stage of opening up
Letting people love her define feminine energy
Be able to just exist in her whole body

She will dye it
Dye white for the snow before the orange makes the new trees grow
Some days she'll wake up to the cat's scratch and feel an itch
Some days if colored blond will the curls stay ready for today's day
Even lead it to water, curl it defined
The days sunshine can drain it tired

And it will move slow
Maybe want to stay hidden under wrap or hoodie in the snow
But that's to be expect when you cut a living things fro
Just to realize that all healthy things will grow
And that's just all it is
Another pivoting point in her define feminine

IX

You're going back to someone because you're not over the feeling or you want to try to fix what is already broken. You say you want closure and that's understandable but you're forgetting that you've had tons of relationships that ended with unsaid words. This is no different.

IX

She had more love and all he had was the cup.
Who knew it was cracked.

IX

Darling a weed that is cut down and stepped on
Is still as pretty as a white rose
Best when wanted and loved, not poisoned- yes!
But dandelion you're surely going to flower

IX

While truth sets the flowers free
Lies still water unwanted seeds

Eeyore Socks

Beauty
It's hard to define it
I don't want to spend my whole life trying to find it
And it's not that I find myself ugly but that sometimes don't know how pretty I am in the streets
As a black women seen to be tamed and clean
Not kept if my clothes ain't ironed and edges ain't stay against my pretty face
However, I no longer define my physical beauty in my hair
Don't want to be so high maintenance that I feel nasty in the mirror when my face is bare
I don't know, I'm giving myself a hard time and I know why… funny enough it's actually because I want to run away
But it's gonna take some more days to finally feel safe
Some more months to get my head to slow it's fast pace
And a few more years to finally get out of this hell whole place
When I do it'll mean the world to celebrate my birthday, holidays, cook,
dance and sweep the floors of my brand new space

Tomorrow brings me closer to hugging
the dreams that made me live to see today

MISCARRIAGE AWARENESS

{little orsetto}

IX

"it's not your fault"

Sunflower

I can't tell you my life.
Can't explain the escape, the way I planned for five years to have a child to a guy, don't know who the guy is but in a way I miss the baby that will never be here.
So, to you I say- wait…
For me as a mother I am for many, called "mom" and acted like one because I didn't have any. However, it wasn't an act but a reflection of the responsibility that was forced upon me that even when not wanting to take, had to take anyway.
Now a trauma response of feeling like I'd be one in a few years from that last painful day.
Then I lost you… Lost it.
Now I lay awake and think, how would the days be with you stink? My very own sunflower whose hair I wash in the sink.
To my maybe.
To my mind and body given away in the form of a baby who didn't get to see the sun from the window, a cry that I would never close the door on because those watering eyes can go to moisturizing the soul…
A sunflower that will one day realize that the love from me is something they no longer need to point their face at to see.
So, here's to my maybe.
That sunflower of a baby.

Braiding Hair

Still young enough to be confused yet old enough to know I can have you
Left to dreaming of braiding your hair to watching you tie your shoe
Teaching you how to sweep and set boundaries in your youth
I don't have a safe place with my parents but shall show you one in me
Darling I will smile as you jump in puddles and sleep to the stories I read

I will give you more than the bare minimum for you are a human with needs
You'll have unconditional love, cooking, hugs, and peace to accept yourself before you ever need to
You will never understand the fear I had coming home or going to sleep
My painful past that I was forced into that made me realize I couldn't have you
My mother is unemotional, and father was distant then
He didn't see family the way he did work and she didn't want me so I was left to learn the pain in how to forgive- alone… but…

When you lay on me do you feel the way my heart beats calmer with you?
Staring into each other's eyes, can you see where my past aches and hides?

No one talks about that feeling. The feeling when you plan to have a child and lose them before seeing them smile. The plan becomes nothing but a dream and as a woman you are expected to pick up as if nothing happened. As if you didn't lose a piece of you. I'm talking to the mothers who wanted their kids but something in the body made them- die. And you still had to push something out that would have been alive. Then wake up the next morning to work that 9 to 5.

No one talks about how the nursery room that once was going to be housed has to be walked past because you can't bare to walk in and take it down. Perhaps you may try again but it won't replace that loss.

No one talks about the way you spend months feeling worthless and uncapable to being pregnant. Being a parent. How those baby names won't have a baby and you slowly start to fear your capabilities. So, you may drown yourself in the bottle filled with this new broken reality.

Cutting yourself against the words of:
"Can I even carry."
"Can I even be there."

You don't owe anyone a relationship with your kids. They are not promised a hug, a visit or your child knowing their name. Especially when they didn't choose to have a healthy relationship with you.

Se vere non lo so

She never feared pregnancy until she went through loss. Now trying to figure out if she can or if loss will happen again. It sends her on a spin cycle not knowing if she can calm down her fears enough to make a decision.

But she walks…
Around an apartment complex, alone, looking at the peaceful white homes thinking of how she would be happier. More peaceful living on her own in a home filled with sun, earth and moon tones. How she wants to go to the pool and take a swim or lean over the side. Reading poetry against the concrete as her baby sits in the chair- close. Playing with a toy while no one else is nearby. In a little towel hoodie covering their tiny curly head.

She slowly climbs out of the water as her child starts to walk her way. Holding out her hand to say "up up" so she picks her up and rests her feet in the shallow end. Her baby in her lap resting her head on her mother's shoulder. And she smiles knowing that she'll be tired and well ready to sleep the rest of the day.

She hears a creek and glances up at the gate. Nothing. So, she looks back and her smile fades from her face.

You're gone from her lap. Toy and towel nowhere to be placed. And she realizes again you weren't there. You are something she can't tell how she wants… she doesn't want you to be another loss orsetto.

IX

…e adesso puoi restare?

Frassi Scritte per meta

They say sometimes souls don't stay long enough to be born because they fulfilled there purpose enough to leave
Maybe that's why their hand you could never squeeze
But in your reality it's not… it's because part of you tried hard to send them away that you took hits to your own body so that they really couldn't stay
If they had managed to then y'all would have had to run away and they would have been raised on the streets
But you were terrified to leave your family for what if they had found you?
What if you didn't run away far enough and had to explain that baby?
You didn't want them to know but that secret wasn't the deepest reason- it was you knowing that your child would have endured all the pain and abuse you had to take
Couldn't bare the thought of knowing that you couldn't protect them if you couldn't even protect yourself.
You were so very young-
-pause-
You were too young to be put in the position of having to even consider having a child. Knowing that they would have been raised alone and you would have to finish raising yourself on your own.

I didn't know how deep my grieving was until I realized that a lot of my depression is heavy in the season of what would have been claimed by you.
-acceptance was the hardest stage-

Stuck in a cycle of hearing people around me telling me that their three-year-old daughter said: "Mommy you're my best friend." I just hope these people lay on the beach realizing that the purest love they could ever hold fits in their hands.

Dear, Universe

I want a healthy baby.
Want them to have a pure heart, my eyes and a unique smile.
But I'm scared for pregnancy. Scared that I may lose them or worse they'd have to grow up without me.
And I can't have that, it would crush me more than losing them would because I don't want the world to raise them.
I want to.
But either way I'm scared so please just let us be okay
I know I'm saying this as if I'm pregnant. Part of me is like "could my body ever be good enough." Just send me a sign. Help me from above for my possible future!
I'm asking for you to make sure my baby and I are healthy for a long while after the fact. I will handle the rest.

- Anonymous

Teach your child to be a good friend.
Not every kid is able to go home to love.

IX

Your kid is learning how to be a person by watching you.
Don't think you're failing because you're not meeting deadlines or you forget to wash clothes when the baby stayed up and cried. Being a mother brings the possibility of a life-long connection in 18 short summers.

It's wild because you wake up, take care of a home, and just do the damn thing. All while making society think it's so easy.
You should be proud mama.
Even the strongest women need to rest. You are carrying a household on your chest.

IX

Your body starts growing
Craving the weirdest things
Laying awake and thinking of what new life will bring
Then the red rushes down like a waterfall
Body bending to the ache
Part of you slowly being stripped away
Your almost new life plan turns to air
Most wouldn't understand that it hurt
Your love remaining nothing but unspoken words

IX

You're one of the harder things I never talk about
Dealt with the pain, the plan, the thoughts, the tears myself as I did everything else. But since I never held your hand you never were able to learn my pain. I want you to know that you have and will always be my biggest push. My biggest:
"Thank you for letting me learn that!"

Drink some tea my love.
You never know how strong you are until it's your only choice.
It's a process but if you are going through this alone allow yourself to feel what you feel. Take as much time as you need to process and distance yourself. Don't obligate yourself to go outside in fear of missing out but take walks to clear your head. Light candles in remembrance to honor what's now dead. Take the day off. Plant a tree. Journal. Eat well, try new foods and remember to get some sleep.

---you will get through this. It will get easier to cope---

IX

Some things in life will impact you for the rest of it. Not everything will come as pain but when it does there is no guarantee how long it may stay. With grief of loss, you can try to make sure you have a safe group of family and friends who will be there to catch you when you fall. But if you're alone then perhaps put some pillows on the floor. Nothing could have prepared you for this fall so take your time. Don't let anyone tell you how to process your pain.

“it’s not my fault”

Read that again

Provide less financial dents

I can sit here and give you every one of the 65 questions I've written down to answer on if having a kid is possible. Or I can give you the top things I said to know I'm ready:

- Having space for a child
- Self-control/ learning to close your open wounds
- Time to give & share
- You are making income

I can sit here and give you every one of the 65 questions I've written down in preparation for having a child. From pregnancy to lifestyle. Yet, it still won't change that once your list is finished and you're done walking down that baby aisle- that you are willing to try again for a child.

IX

Guess I must wait another lifetime to meet you. There I won't be in the same body but here- I'm still grieving because I made it through. Now I know that I can finally have a you. Give them safety were my own life failed you… I just don't know if I'd be blessed to have a tiny hand to hold or extra shoes by the door, I have to remind them to take to practice once more.

IX

"Congratulations on a healthy baby!"

"Not until 12 weeks."

"I said your baby is healthy."

"Won't survive the first winter."

"Listen to me… your baby is healthy my love!"

In the deepest part of my heart, there you are. Planting flowers and dancing in the rain. Making me soft to the naked eye.

"*It won't be easy*"
She knows
But it wasn't easy letting go
Trying again feels like sitting waiting for the flat line to kick in
She hangs up a sunflower painting in a nursery room in remembering old wounds
But as her stomach grows her throat feels closed, choking on her own "I don't know"
Taking care of life isn't new but to bring one in now is its own puzzle book
Will she fail? Will they be close? Will her kid grow up and never want to come back home?
Fears fill her chest as she tries to take deep breaths
Looking into her empty nursery to remind her that family is only two months away-

IX

She clocks into a job she'd rather not go to
Feeling the same walking through a door
        of a home she'd rather not live in
Thinking of the bruises and fights she alone had to carry
Barely holding on
Barely letting go
Barely allowing herself to fill the black hole of her soul

She clocks into a job she'd rather not go to
Making money she'd rather spend on creating something
        she'd want to come home for
To let the bruises and fights wash themselves away
Yet not holding on
Not letting go
Not allowing herself to see that the hole isn't a vast void

She clocks into a job she'd rather not go to
Every time she's on the way home she'd have to stop by the daycare to
        cradle her kid in her arms
Bruises and fights eventually healed
Always holding on
Always being protective
Always choosing to learn more so she can teach better lessons

IX

~ for those who are lost, this will find you~

And that's what it feels like. Magic almost.
To find something written for you in a time you
most relate. Almost as if you wrote it yourself, the
words flow from another as if they picked your
brain miles away

IX

IX

www.ingramcontent.com/pod-product-compliance
Lightning Source LLC
Chambersburg PA
CBHW021132020426
42331CB00005B/732
* 9 7 9 8 2 1 8 2 5 6 7 7 7 *